Why does Mary wear blue?

CTS Children's Books

Contents

Text by: Pierpaolo Finaldi

Illustrations by: Ettore & Mattia Finaldi and the children of Year 5, Holy Cross School, Catford.

Pictures: Cover Image: Courtesy of Monastero di Vallechiara, Lanuvio, Rome. Page 1: *Virgin and Child* by Sassoferrato © The Gallery Collection/Corbis. Page 3: *Madonna and Child statue* in Quebec city's Notre-Dame-des-victoires church. Early 19th century © Nicolas McComber/istockphoto. Page 5: *Presentation of the Virgin in the Temple* by Philippe de Champaigne © The Gallery Collection/Corbis. Page 7: *The Annunciation* by Fra Angelico © The Gallery Collection/Corbis. Page 9: *Detail of Holy Family from The Nativity of Jesus Christ* by Giotto di Bordone © Alinari Archives/CORBIS. Page 11: *Bernadette Soubirous*, from a late 19th century painting (tinted photo mounted on card), French School, (20th century) / Bibliotheque des Arts Decoratifs, Paris, France / Archives Charmet / The Bridgeman Art Library. Page 13: *Immaculate Conception* by Guido Reni © Alinari Archives/CORBIS. Page 15: *The Wilton Diptych. Front view of the Wilton Diptych*, depicting Richard II presented to the Virgin and Child by his patron Saint John the Baptist and Saints Edward and Edmund © The Gallery Collection/Corbis. Page 17: *Pilgrims pray outside of the basilica of Notre-Dame des Douleurs where Pope Benedict XVI gives mass and adminster unction to the sick on his last day in Lourdes*, 2008 © Guillaume Horcajuelo/epa/Corbis. Page 18: *Madonna and Child with the Infant Saint John* by Giovanni Della Robbia © Arte & Immagini srl/CORBIS. Page 19: *Eastern Icon of the Madonna and child with God the Father and angels* © Amal Sajdak/istockphoto. Page 21: *The Immaculate Conception*, 1767-1769 (oil on canvas), Tiepolo, Giovanni Battista (Giambattista) (1696-1770) / Prado, Madrid, Spain / Photo © AISA / The Bridgeman Art Library. Page 23: *Dormition of the Virgin* by Fra Angelico © Philadelphia Museum of Art/CORBIS.

Questions: Special thanks go to Miss Collins and all the children of Year 5 in Holy Cross School, Catford, London.

Why does Mary wear Blue?: Published 2010 by the Incorporated Catholic Truth Society, 40-46 Harleyford Road, London SE11 5AY. Tel: 020 7640 0042; Fax: 020 7640 0046; www.cts-online.org.uk. Copyright © 2010 The Incorporated Catholic Truth Society.

ISBN: 978 1 86082 694 8   CTS Code CH 30

'Mother of Jesus and Our Mother'!

Jesus is the Son of God and the Son of Mary. He is our brother and he gave Mary to all of us to be out Mother too. To really learn to love Our Lady, we need to get to know her. This book answers some of the questions asked by children about our Blessed Mother. She is always there to help us and wants all her children to talk to her in prayer and to visit her as often as possible. So when you go to Church or School stop for a moment in front of her statue and say hello, and try to visit one of her many shrines around the world where Mary is always ready to welcome all her children, especially you!

This book was written answering questions asked by the children of Year 5 in Holy Cross School in Catford, South East London.

Who were Mary's parents?

Mary was probably born and grew up in Jerusalem. It is said that her father was called Joachim and he was a shepherd who provided sheep for the sacrifices at the temple in Jerusalem. We are told that Mary's mother was called Anna. We do not know a lot about them but there are many beautiful paintings of one event in their lives.

Usually Jewish parents only took their firstborn sons to the temple in Jerusalem and presented them to God, but Mary's parents knew their daughter was special, so they took her to the temple too! Ever since the night when God struck down the first born of Egypt and spared the children of Israel every Jewish firstborn child belonged in a special way to God.

In Egypt God had saved the people of Israel from slavery, but with the help of Mary he was about to save the whole world from sin and death!

Who were Mary's parents?

Why was Mary chosen to be the Mother of God ?

Every one of us has been chosen by God to do some special job that only we can do. We are free to say yes to God or to say no to his plan and do only what we want. It is a mystery why God chooses us, but he always has a plan to help us and the people around us to get to heaven.

In Mary's case God had been planning to save all of mankind from the beginning of time. She had been prepared from before her birth for the great task that God would ask her to do. God wanted to show how much he loved the human beings he had created by becoming one of them. He wanted his son to be born from a woman just like every other child.

When the Archangel Gabriel asked Mary if she wanted to be the mother of the son of God she was full of fear but trusted God and said yes. Her 'yes' was what made Mary worthy to be the Mother of God!

Why was Mary chosen to be the mother of God?

Did **Mary** have any other **children?**

The Holy Family was made up of three people: Jesus, Mary and Joseph. When the Gospels mention the 'brothers of Jesus' they are probably speaking about his cousins or other close family. When Mary agreed to be the Mother of Jesus and Joseph accepted the job of looking after them, they knew that they had been asked to do something truly amazing. From the moment that Jesus began to grow in Mary's womb, Mary and Joseph looked after Jesus and did everything they could to help him in his mission to save everyone in the world. They dedicated their lives completely to the job that God had asked them to do. Joseph must have died when Jesus was a young man but Mary stayed near Jesus until he went up to heaven.

When Jesus was about to die on the Cross he gave Mary a new family and lots more children. He wanted the Apostle John and all Christians including you and me to call Mary our mother.

Why has Mary appeared to people like St Bernadette and the three children in Fatima?

Mary loves all of her children and throughout history has looked for new ways to show her love. One special way has been to visit and speak to some very unexpected people in some very surprising places.

In 1521 Mary appeared in Guadalupe in Mexico to a poor man who had only recently been baptised. He was called Juan Diego and she told him that she wanted a shrine to be built where she could show her love to everyone. From that moment onwards people from all over the Americas have gone to pray at her shrine in Guadalupe and many miracles have taken place there.

In 1858 in Lourdes, in France, Mary appeared to a poor girl called Bernadette and told her to pray for sinners and to drink from a spring of water and to wash in it. Now millions of people each year go to Lourdes to pray and to wash in the waters. Many sick people have been healed of their illnesses.

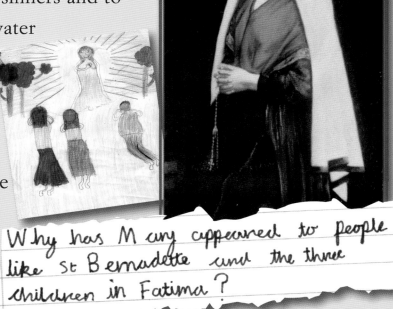

Why has Mary appeared to people like St Bernadette and the three children in Fatima?

In 1917, during the First World War, Mary appeared to three children whose names were Lucia, Jacinta and Francisco in Fatima in Portugal. They were poor shepherds and one day while they were looking after their sheep, Mary appeared to them and told them to pray the Rosary for peace in the world and for sinners to change. They prayed and passed on Mary's messages and have helped many people.

Why is Mary called the Immaculate Conception?

When Mary appeared to Bernadette in Lourdes she told her that she was the 'Immaculate Conception'. Bernadette did not know what this meant but she repeated what Mary had said. The word immaculate means clean and without a stain, and the stain we are talking about in this case is original sin. From the moment that Mary began to grow in her mother's womb and all through her life she remained without any sin, even original sin. Original sin is what has been passed on to every human being from the moment Adam and Eve disobeyed God in the Garden of Eden by eating the fruit even though God had told them not to. Original sin has one very sad effect; it means that like Adam and Eve we are more likely to give in to temptation than to do what God asks us to do. God wanted Mary to be born without original sin so that when he asked her to be the Mother of his Son, she would be able to make up her own mind. She said 'yes' to God and for this reason she is honoured by every generation.

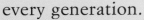

Why is Mary called the Immaculate Conception?

Why do we pray to Mary?

We pray using Mary's words when we say the Magnificat: 'My soul proclaims the greatness of the Lord!' We praise Mary using the words of the angel in the Gospel when we say 'Hail Mary, full of grace' and ask her to pray for us now and at the hour of our death.

We know that Mary is in heaven with her son Jesus and all the other Saints who have died. We also know that Mary has a special place in heaven, she is the Queen of heaven and is always shown sitting next to her son. When Jesus was on earth his mother was able to persuade him to perform miracles even when he didn't really want to! At the wedding at Cana when the wine ran out, Mary wanted her son to help and even though he said it was not his hour, he helped the bride and groom by turning water into wine.

When we pray to Mary we are asking her to pass on our request to Jesus who is near her and listens to her. She loves us all as a mother and is always ready to listen to our prayers and put in a good word for us with her son for whom nothing is impossible.

Why do we pray to Mary?

Why do we say so many Hail Marys in the Rosary?

The Rosary is a very old and beautiful prayer. In it we say 1 Our Father then 10 Hail Marys and at the same time we think about an important moment in the life of Jesus, like his birth or his crucifixion. We can use rosary beads to help us keep count of the number of Our Fathers and Hail Marys that we say while we think about the mysteries of Jesus' life.

Saying the Hail Mary helps us not to get distracted and brings our minds closer to our Blessed Mother. She knew Jesus better than anyone else and shared in all the most important moments of his life.

Praying the rosary is like a school where we sit at Mary's feet and we learn from her how much Jesus loves us, what he is like and all the wonderful things he did for us.

Why do we say so many Hail Marys in the Rosary?

Why does Mary wear blue?

Mary is called the most beautiful of all women. But her beauty does not come from her clothes. It comes from the fact that she is full of grace, that she has never sinned and that she gave us Jesus. How can we show such beauty in pictures and statues? We must use symbols and colours to help as well. Blue is the colour of the sky and it reminds us that Mary is in heaven. The Bible says that Mary was clothed with the sun.

We cannot look at the sun but we know it is sunny when the sky is blue. Blue is also the colour of the sea and of water, and Mary is sometimes called the Star of the Sea. Water is pure and used to wash things clean, and Mary was the purest of God's creatures. White is also used to represent purity and Mary often wears a white dress with a blue cloak or veil on top. In icons like the one on this page, Mary is always shown wearing red and blue. Red is the colour of royalty and shows that Mary is the Queen of Heaven who gave birth to Jesus the King of the Universe.

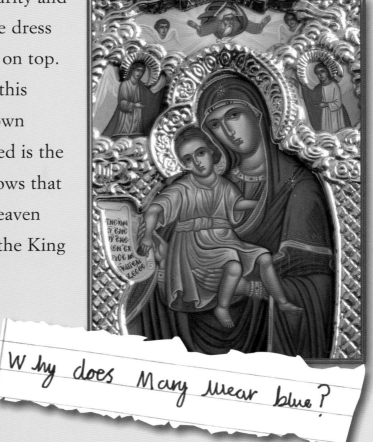

Why does Mary wear blue?

Why is Mary sometimes shown standing on a serpent?

At the beginning of the Bible we read about Adam and Eve, they were happy in the Garden of Eden and lived in love and peace with God. God had told them not to eat the fruit from the tree in the middle of the garden but the serpent spoke to Eve and tempted her to disobey God. He told her that God did not really love her and wanted to stop her from doing things that were good. Eve believed the serpent and ate the fruit and Adam did too. This was the first sin, and meant that Adam and Eve had to leave the garden of Eden and live and die on earth and suffer during their lives.

Death and sin had come into the world through a woman who had listened to the serpent. God wanted to save the people he had created so he decided to send another woman who would listen to him and not the

serpent. That woman was Mary. She listened to God and obeyed him and gave birth to our Saviour Jesus. She did not listen to the serpent, who is the devil, and her son defeated the devil, so she is often shown crushing the serpent under her feet.

Why is Mary somtimes shown standing on a serpent?

How did Mary die?

We do not know much about Mary's life or death after the day of Pentecost when she was in the Upper Room with the disciples. Tradition tells us that after Jesus's ascension Mary went to live with the Apostle John in Jerusalem or in a city called Ephesus, which is in modern Turkey. Mary lived to a good age and when she had done everything that God had asked of her during her life she was taken up to heaven, body and soul.

We do not know if Mary died and then went to heaven or if she was taken up to heaven before she died. The Christians in the East believe that Mary fell asleep and her body was taken up to heaven as she slept so they do not speak of her death but of her 'dormition' or 'falling asleep'. Others believe that she died and was then taken up to heaven. What we do know for certain is that she went to heaven and was crowned by Jesus as Queen of Heaven and she sits with him listening to our prayers and interceding for us with God and her son Jesus.

How did Mary die?

CTS Children's Books